BERRY FIN

A Guide to Native Plants with Fleshy Fruits
for Eastern North America

DORCAS S. MILLER
illustrated by CHERIE HUNTER DAY

Nature Study
Guild Publishers
an imprint of AdventureKEEN

START HERE

This book will help you identify plants with fleshy fruit or colorful but dry fruit in the shape of a berry, drupe, multiple, or other form.

To use the book, start by reviewing p. 1–3.

When examining your plant, note the color and form of the mature fruit, as well as the position and shape of the leaves.

Go to the entry key on p. 4, make a choice, and go on from there. At the section keys, consider all the factors—margin of leaf, fruit color, position of fruit, height, range, and other clues.

Area of coverage

Names: This book uses scientific and common names from the database of the Integrated Taxonomic Information System. If you prefer a different name, feel free to add it in the margin.

Color describes the mature fruit. Most unripe fruit is green or white, and it may turn several colors before maturing.

Range: If a species is found in one part of a state, the entire state is included.

N: Northern	**TH:** Throughout	**Northeast:** PA, NJ, NY, New England
S: Southern	**~TH:** Mostly throughout	**Midwest:** MO, IL, IN, OH north
E: Eastern	**Mts:** Appalachians	**NB:** New Brunswick; **Que:** Quebec
W: Western	**NE:** New England	**Ont:** Ontario

© 2024, 1996, 1986 Dorcas S. Miller (text), Cherie Hunter Day (illustrations); · ISBN 978-0-912550-52-7 · Printed in China · Cataloging-in-Publication data is available from the Library of Congress · naturestudy.com

Berry Finder provides identification information for more than 180 species with berries or berry-like fruit. Some fruits in this book are delicious, some are disagreeable, some are dangerous, and some are deadly. The inclusion of a plant here implies neither edibility nor toxicity. Both foragers and nonforagers can profit by using these eight keys, which are designed to help you identify plants in the wild. As you identify, be curious, cautious, and prudent.

A good foraging guide, on the other hand, contains information regarding identifying, harvesting, and safely preparing wild fruit. It offers details about poisonous plants, plants that cause dermatitis, and poisonous plants that might be mistaken for nonpoisonous plants.

ABBREVIATIONS

W: White	**Fr:** fruit
Y: Yellow	**Lf:** Leaf
O: Orange	**Lvs:** Leaves
R: Red	**Lflt:** Leaflet
P: Purple	**Opp:** Opposite
Blu: Blue	**Alt:** Alternate
Bla: Black	**Sm:** Small
G: Green	

Parentheses 2–5" (–7") Plant 2–5" high but can grow to 7"

(Y) R   Fruit usually red, but can be yellow

Glaucous: A whitish (or bluish) waxy covering; or, more generally, any whitish surface

 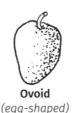

Spherical	**Ovoid**	**Ellipsoid**	**Cylindric**
	(egg-shaped)	*(widest in middle)*	*(parallel sided)*

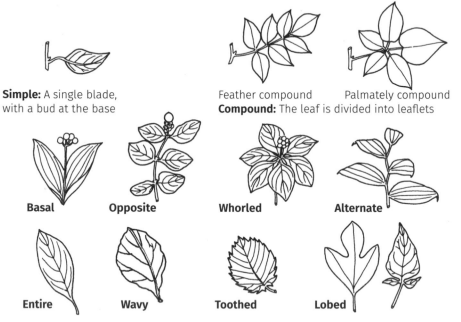

Simple: A single blade, with a bud at the base

Feather compound

Palmately compound

Compound: The leaf is divided into leaflets

Basal

Opposite

Whorled

Alternate

Entire

Wavy

Toothed

Lobed

FRUIT

Terminal **Axillary:** Originating between leaf and stem **In an umbel** **In a raceme** **In a panicle**

Berry
Soft seeds embedded in fruit (*e.g., blueberry*)

Drupe
Fleshy portion encloses stone; seed inside stone (e.g., *plum, cherry*)

Hip
Leathery sac with few to many seeds (e.g., *rose*)

Pome
Flesh encloses papery inner wall; seeds inside (e.g., *apple*)

Accessory
Small, hard seeds lie on surface of flesh (e.g., *strawberry*)

Aggregate
Many small fruits surround a central receptacle (e.g., *raspberry*)

ENTRY KEY

Using the images on p. 2–3, choose the description that best matches your plant.

	Page
A vine (a plant that climbs by tendrils, aerial rootlets, or a twining stem)	5
A low-growing or prostrate plant to ~7" high	12
An herb with parallel-veined leaves	14
leaves not parallel-veined	18
no visible veins (Asparagus, below)	
A woody plant with opposite leaves	26
alternate leaves	36
evergreen needles or palms	58–59

Asparagus, *Asparagus officinialis*
Leaves are inconspicuous scales; the branches are the small, green, veinless structures that appear to be leaves.
Fr R; H to 6.5'; TH

KEY: VINES

Climbs by	W	Y	O	R	P	Blu	Bla	Tendrils grow		Page
Tendrils							Bla	Opposite palmately compound lf	**Virginia creeper**	6
					P	Blu	Bla	Opposite compound lf	**Peppervine**	6–7
		Amber		R	P	Blu	Bla	Opposite simple lf	**Grape**	7
		Specked; various colors						Opposite deeply lobed lf	**Porcelainberry**	6
				R	P	Blu	Bla	From base of lf stem	**Carrionflower, greenbriar**	8
								Leaves		
Twining stem				R			Bla	Opposite	**Honeysuckle**	9
						Blu		Alt, entire; fr oval or oblong	**Supplejack**	9
				R		Blu	Bla	Alt, entire to 3–lobed	**Moonseed**	10
							Bla	Alt, 3–7 lobed	**Cupseed**	10
				R				Alt; fr in yellow jacket	**Bittersweet**	11
Aerial rootlets							Bla	Alt, lobed; fr in umbel	**English ivy**	11
	~W	~Y						3 shiny lflts *Don't touch!*	**Poison ivy**	54
Sprawls for support				R				Alt lobed	**Bitter nightshade**	21

Fruit	Leaves	Margin		Range
Amber, R, P, blu, bla	Simple	Toothed; some lobed	**Grape**, *Vitis* spp	TH
			Parthenocissus	
Bla	Palmately compound	Toothed	**Virginia creeper**, *P. quinquefolia*	TH
			Ampelopsis	
P	Simple	Some slightly lobed	**Heartleaf peppervine**, *A. cordata*	S ⅔
Dark P–bla	Feather compound		**Peppervine**, *A. arborea*	S ½
Speckled; W, blu, Bla, cream, pink, lavender	Simple	May be lobed	**Porcelainberry**, *A. glandulosa* Invasive; locally dense (not illustrated)	Scattered states

Virginia creeper

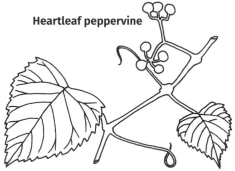

Heartleaf peppervine

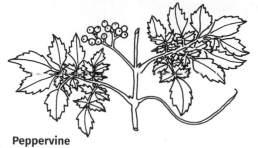

Peppervine

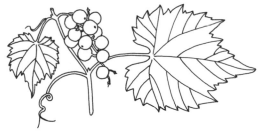

Riverbank grape

Fruit	Lobed	Grape *Vitis*	Range
Dark P–bla	Yes	**Summer,** *V. aestivalis*	TH
Bla	Yes	**Riverbank,** *V. riparia*	TH (not AL, GA, FL, SC)
Nearly bla	Mostly not	**Graybark,** *V. cinerea*	S ⅔
Bla	Mostly not	**Frost,** *V. vulpina*	TH (not MN, WI, NE)
R, blu, P	No	**Muscadine,** *V. rotundifolia*	S ½

CATBRIAR FAMILY: Tendrils; fruit in umbels; veins follow margin edges, lvs alternate

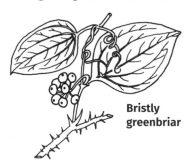

Bristly greenbriar

Smooth carrionflower

Fruit	Herbaceous	Prickles	Carrionflower	_Smilax_	Height/ length	Range
Dark blu, glaucous	Yes	Yes	**Smooth,**	S. herbacea	to 8'	TH
Blu, almost bla	Yes	Yes	**Blue Ridge.,**	S. lasioneura	to 5'	AR–MN N; Midwest
	Woody		**Greenbriar**			
Bla, not glaucous	Evergreen	Yes	**Bristly,**	S. hispida	to 25'	TH
P to bla	Evergreen	Yes	**Laurel,**	S. laurifolia	to 16+'	S ⅓
R	Deciduous	Few	**Coral,**	S. walteri	to 20'	S ⅓
Bla, usually glaucous	Deciduous to semi-evergreen	Yes	**Common,**	S. rotundifolia	to 40'	TH

HONEYSUCKLE FAMILY
Twining; woody; except Japanese, joined upper leaves

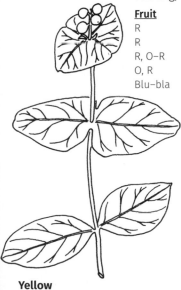

Fruit	Honeysuckle _Lonicera_*	Height	Range
R	**Trumpet,** L. sempervirens	10–20'	Mostly S ½
R	**Grape,** L reticulata	10–15'	Mostly Midwest
R, O–R	**Limber,** L. diocia	6' (–10')	N ⅔
O, R	**Yellow,** L. flava	10–20'	Mostly AL, AR, MO
Blu-bla	**Japanese,** L. japonica	15–30'	TH

*Species with widest distribution

**Yellow
honeysuckle**

Supplejack
Alabama, _Berchemia scandens_
Fr blu, oval or oblong; H to 60'; S ½

Twining

Carolina moonseed

Canada moonseed

Cupseed leaf

Fruit	Leaves	Lf stem attaches to	Plant		Height	Range
R	Entire to 3–lobed	Lf margin	Woody	**Carolina moonseed,** *Cocculus carolinus*	to 10'	S ½
Bla	Entire to 3–lobed	Lf undersurface	Woody	**Canada moonseed,** *Menispermum canadense*	to 12'	TH
Bla	3–7 lobed	Lf margin	Herbaceous	**Cupseed,** *Calycocarpum lyoni*	to 60'	S ½

BITTERSWEET: Twining;
Asian species highly invasive;
the two species hybridize

IVIES: Aerial rootlets
English ivy, *Hedera helix*
Fr bla, in umbel; lvs lobed; H 20–30'; TH
Poison ivy, see p. 54

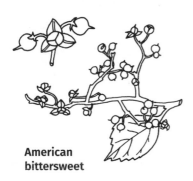

**American
bittersweet**

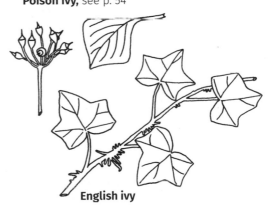

English ivy

Bittersweet: Bright red fruit in yellow jacket in both species

Fruit		Notes	*Bittersweet* *Celastrus*	Height	Range
R; Y shell	2–3 in axil	Introduced	**Asian,** *C. orbiculatus*	to 60'	TH
R; Y shell	Terminal cluster	Native	**American,** *C. scandens*	20' (–30')	TH

Lf evergreen, see p. 58.
Upright plant, see p. 16.

Indica mockstrawberry
Seeds raised above
surface; invasive

Wild strawberry: Seeds in small pits
Woodland, *F. vesca;* seeds on surface; N ⅔

Partridgeberry

Fruit	Leaves		Height	Range
R, juicy, not round	Basal, compound	**Wild strawberry,** *Fragaria virginiana*	4–7"	TH
R, round	Basal, compound	**Indica mockstrawberry,** *Potentilla indica*	3–5"	~TH
R, round, solitary	Opposite	**Partridgeberry,** *Mitchella repens*	2"	N ⅔
R, round	Whorled	**Canada bunchberry,** *Cornus canadensis*	4–8"	N ⅔ (p. 29)

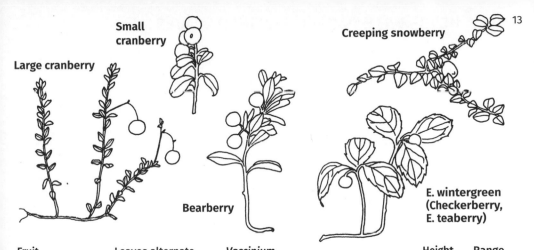

Large cranberry

Small cranberry

Creeping snowberry

Bearberry

E. wintergreen (Checkerberry, E. teaberry)

Fruit	Leaves alternate	*Vaccinium*	Height	Range
R, along stem	Leathery	**Large cranberry,** *V. macrocarpon*	4–6"	N ⅔
R, at tip	Margins rolled under	**Small cranberry,** *V. oxycoccus*	3–5"	N ⅓
R, mealy	Leathery, evergreen	**Bearberry,** *V. uva-ursi*	Prostrate	N ½
		Gaultheria		
R, mealy	Entire/sm round teeth	**Eastern wintergreen,** *G. procumbens*	4–8"	TH
W, mealy	Entire	**Creeping snowberry,** *G. hispida*	Prostrate	TH
Dark R, aggregate	Compound/toothed	**Dwarf red raspberry,** *Rubus pubescens*	4–6"	N ⅔ (p. 52)

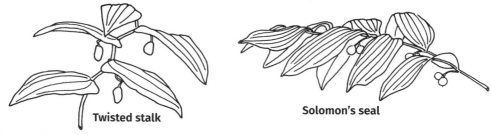

Twisted stalk

Solomon's seal

Stem arching; fruit

			Height	Range	Page
R	Hangs singly	**Twisted stalk,** *Streptopus* spp	to 3'	N ⅓	Above
R	Hangs in pair	**Solomon's seal,** *Polyganatum* spp	to 4.5'	TH	Above
R	Terminal panicle	**False Solomon's seal,** *Maianthemum,* spp.	varies	TH	15
R	2 berries at tip	**Fairybells,** *Prosartes* spp	1.3–3'	E US	15
Tan	3-lobed	**Nodding mandarin,** *P. maculata* (not illus)	to 2.5'	M ⅓	—

Plant upright (p. 16)

R	Lvs alt on stem	**Canada mayflower,** *Maianthemum canadense*	2–8"	TH	16
R	Lvs at base	**European lily of the valley,** *Convallaria majalis*	4–8"	TH	16
Bla	Bulbets in axils	**Tiger lily,** *Lilium lancifolium*	2–4'	~TH	16
Bla	Aggregate	**Blackberry lily,** *Belacandra chinenis*	1–2'	S ¾	17
Blu/bla	Umbel	**Blue bead lily,** *Clintonia* spp	6–12"	N ⅔	17
P/bla	Umbel	**Cucumber-root,** *Medeola virginiana*	1–3'	TH	17

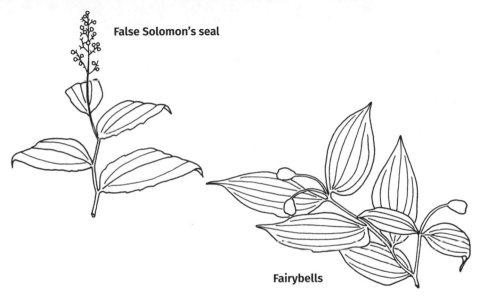

False Solomon's seal

Fairybells

*Trillium (p. 19) has leaf veins that follow the margin and are somewhat paralell-veined.

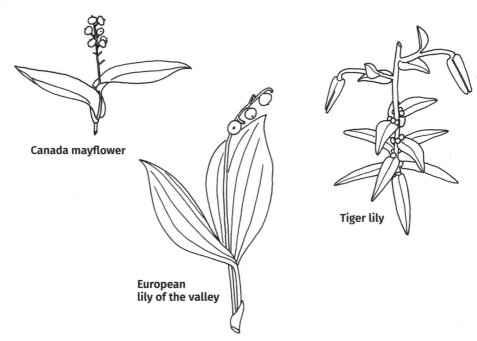

Canada mayflower

European
lily of the valley

Tiger lily

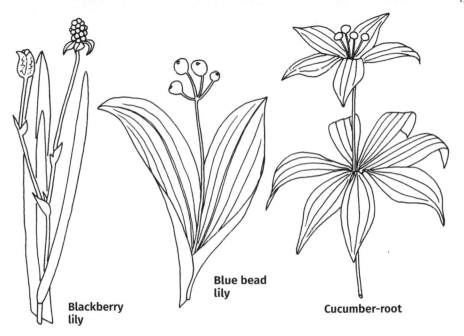

Blackberry lily

Blue bead lily

Cucumber-root

Leaves	W	Y	O	R	P	Blu	Bla	Fruit		Page
Simple										
Whorled		Pale gr		R	P			Solitary; 3 leaves	**Trillium**	19
				R				Tightly clustered; 6 lvs	**Bunchberry**	29
Opposite		Y–O						Solitary or cluster in axil	**Horse-gentian**	19
Alt entire							Bla	Button-like, raceme	**Pokeweed**	19
Alt wavy, toothed or lobed				R				Small, dense cluster	**Strawberry blight**	20
			O–R					Aggregate, solitary	**Goldenseal**	20
		Y–O						Enclosed in papery sac	**Ground cherry**	20
							Bla	In umbel	**Deadly nightshade**	21
				Bright R				Terminal cluster	**Bitter nightshade**	21
		Y						Along stem	**Carolina horsenettle**	21
Basal				R				Dense cluster, fleshy stem	**Wild calla**	24
Compound										
Toothed		Y		R				In single umbel	**Ginsing**	22
					P		Bla	In 2 or more umbels	**Sarsaparilla**	22–23
					P			In panicle	**American spikenard**	23
Entire			O–R					Tight cluster, fleshy stem	**Dragon or Jack**	24
Toothed, lobed	W			R				Raceme	**Baneberry**	25
							Bla	Raceme	**Cohosh**	25

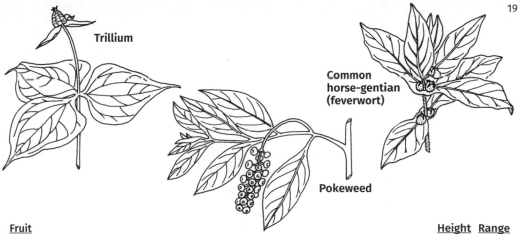

Fruit			**Height**	**Range**
P, lilac, pale G, R, scarlet, maroon	One ovold or spherical	**Trillium,** *Trillium* spp	8–16"	TH
Dark P	Button-like or round berry	**Pokeweed,** *Phytolacca americana*	to 10'	TH
		Horse-gentian *Triostium*		
Dull O–Y	(1–) 3–4 in axil	**Common,** *T. perfoliatum*	to 4.3'	~TH
O–R	As above	**Orangefruit,** *T. aurantiacum*	8"–2.6'	~TH
O–R	Solitary in axil	**Yellowfruit,** *T. angustifolium*	8"–2.6'	~TH

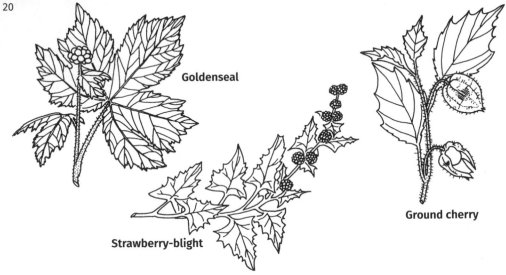

Goldenseal

Ground cherry

Strawberry-blight

Fruit			Height	Range
O–R	Solitary, aggregate	**Goldenseal,** *Hydrastis canadensis*	8–20"	~TH
Bright R	Small, lumpy cluster	**Strawberry-blight,** *Chenopodium capitatum*	8–24"	N ½
R–O, Y, G	Within papery sac	**Ground cherry,** *Physalis* spp	to 3'	TH

NIGHTSHADE FAMILY

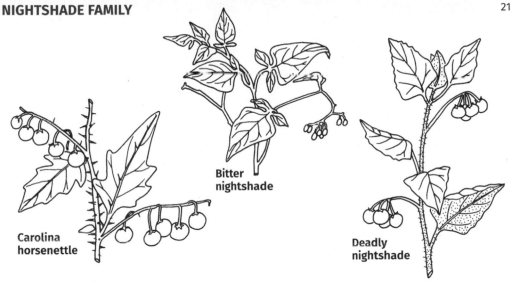

Carolina horsenettle

Bitter nightshade

Deadly nightshade

Fruit	Location	*Solanum*		Height	Range
Bla	In umbels	**Deadly nightshade,** S. nigrum		Erect 6"–2'	Scattered TH
Bright R	Clustered	**Bitter nightshade,** S. dulcamara		Scrambling 3–10'	~N ½
Y	From stem	**Carolina horsenettle,** S. carolinense		Erect 3.5'	TH

GINSENG FAMILY
Fruit in umbels

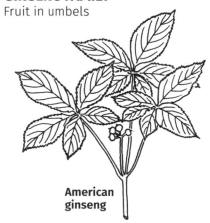

American ginseng

Bristly sarsaparilla

Fruit	Umbels	Ginseng *Panax*	Height	Range
Bright R	Solitary	**American,** *P. quinquefolia*	8"–2'	TH but rare in some areas
Y	Solitary	**Dwarf,** *P. trifolius*	4–8"	N ½, S in mountains
		Sarsaparilla *Aralia*		
Bla	2 or more	**Bristly,** *A. hispida*	to 5'	N ⅓
Bla	2 or more	**Wild,** *A. nudicaulis*	to 1.6'	All but Gulf States, AR
Dark P	2 or more	**American spikenard,** *A. racemosa*	to 10'	N ⅔

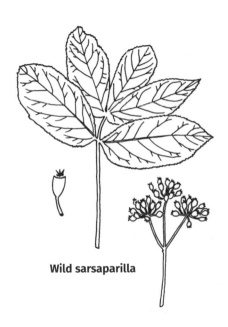

Wild sarsaparilla

American spikenard

ARUM FAMILY
Fruit densely clustered on fleshy stem

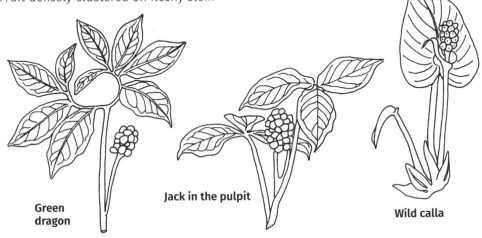

Green dragon

Jack in the pulpit

Wild calla

Fruit	Leaflets		Height	Range
O–R	7–15	**Green dragon,** *Arisaema dracontium*	8–20" (–3')	Mostly TH
O–R	3	**Jack in the pulpit,** *A. tryphillum*	1–3"	TH
R	None	**Wild calla,** *Calla palustris*	4–8"	N ⅓

Both plants with fruit in raceme

Red baneberry

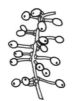

White baneberry
Fruit on thick, red stems

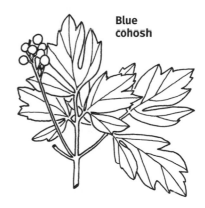

Blue cohosh

Fruit	Shape	Baneberry _Actaea_	Height	Range
R	Round	**Red,** A. rubra	1.3–2.6'	N ⅓
W	Ovid	**White,** A. pachypoda	1.3–2.6'	TH
		Cohosh _Caulophyllum_		
Dark blu	Round	**Blue,** C. thalictrides	1–2.6'	~TH except FL, LA
Blu	Round	**Giant blue,** C. giganteum	to 3'	Mostly N ⅔

Leaves	W	Y	O	R	P	Blu	Bla	Fruit	Notes	Page
Simple										
Entire or wavy	W		Coral		P			Dense cluster, terminal and/or in axils	**Symphoricarpos**	27
Entire	W					Blu	Bla	In broad cluster; lf veins follow margin	**Dogwood**	28
				R				In dense terminal cluster; veins as above	**Flowering dogwood**	28–29
		(Y)		R				Round, no scales; lvs with scales	**Buffaloberry**	30
		Silvery						Ellipsoid; densely covered with scales	**Silverberry**	30
			O	R		Blu	Bla	In pairs in axil	**Honeysuckle**	31
					P		Bla	In axillary panicles; tree	**Devilwood**	32–33
					P		Bla	In axillary clusters; plant thorny	**Swamp-privet**	33
					P	Blu	Bla	In axillary clusters; no thorns	**Fringetree**	33
							Bla	In terminal clusters; shrub	**Wild privet**	33
							Bla	In umbels; spiny twigs	**European buckthorn***	49
Toothed				Rose	P	Blu		Dense clusters on stem; coarse teeth	**Beautyberry**	32
				R	P	Blu	Bla	In umbel-like clusters; drupe, 1 stone	**Viburnum**	34
Lobed				R	P	Blu		In terminal cluster; drupe, 1 stone	**Viburnum**	34
Compound				R	P		Bla	Cluster type varies; drupe, 3–5 stones	**Elderberry**	35

* European buckthorn may have opposite, sub-opposite, and alternate leaves on the same plant.

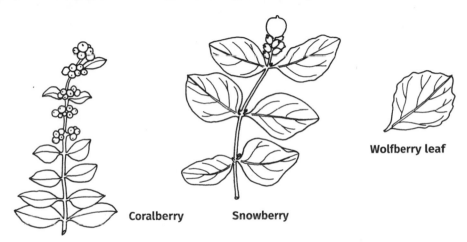

SYMPHORICARPOS: Coralberry, Wolfberry, Snowberry

Coralberry

Snowberry

Wolfberry leaf

Fruit	Tight clusters	Lf margins	*Symphoricarpos*	Height	Range
Coral–P	In axil	Entire	**Coralberry,** *S. orbiculatis*	to 5'	H
W	In axil	Wavy	**Wolfberry,** *S. occidentalis*	to 3.5'	N ½, not NE
W	Terminal	Wavy	**Snowberry,** *S. albus*	to 3.5'	N ½

DOGWOOD FAMILY: Leaf veins follow margin to tip

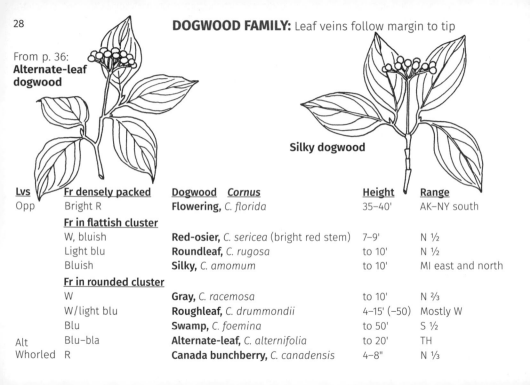

From p. 36:
Alternate-leaf dogwood

Silky dogwood

Lvs	Fr densely packed	Dogwood _Cornus_	Height	Range
Opp	Bright R	**Flowering,** _C. florida_	35–40'	AK–NY south
	Fr in flattish cluster			
	W, bluish	**Red-osier,** _C. sericea_ (bright red stem)	7–9'	N ½
	Light blu	**Roundleaf,** _C. rugosa_	to 10'	N ½
	Bluish	**Silky,** _C. amomum_	to 10'	MI east and north
	Fr in rounded cluster			
	W	**Gray,** _C. racemosa_	to 10'	N ⅔
	W/light blu	**Roughleaf,** _C. drummondii_	4–15' (–50)	Mostly W
	Blu	**Swamp,** _C. foemina_	to 50'	S ½
Alt	Blu–bla	**Alternate-leaf,** _C. alternifolia_	to 20'	TH
Whorled	R	**Canada bunchberry,** _C. canadensis_	4–8"	N ⅓

Flowering dogwood

From p. 18:
Canada bunchberry,
Low-growing, nonwoody

OLEASTER FAMILY: Buffaloberry, "the olives," and silverberry
Leaves with scales

Buffaloberry

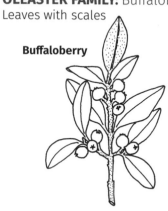

Silverberry
Sometimes invasive;
other *Elaeagnus* highly invasive;
Russian berry scales can be rusty

Fr round	Scales	Buffaloberry *Shepherdia*	Lf scales silvery	Height	Range
Bright R (Y)	None	**Russet,** *S. canadensis*	Lower surface	3.5–10'	N ⅓
Bright R	None	**Silver,** *S. argentia*	Both surfaces	to 20'	N ⅓, not NE

Fr ovoid	Silvery	*Elaeagnus* (from p. 36)			
Silvery	Yes	**Silverberry,** *E. commutata*	Both surfaces	6–16'	MS, PA, NY, MN, Canada
R	Yes	**Autumn olive,** *E. umbellata*	Both surfaces	to 16'	TH
R-brown	Yes	**Thorny olive,** *E. pungens*	Lower surface	to 15'	S ¹⁄₃₂
R-burnt O	Also rusty	**Russian olive,** *E. angustifolia*	Both surfaces	to 20'	TH

SHRUB HONEYSUCKLE, *Lonicera*

Berries may be internally joined or separate.
Fr blu–bla, elongate: **Mountain fly,** *villosa*; 1–5'; N ⅓
Fr R, elongate: **American,** *canadensis*; 2–5'; mostly N ½

American fly

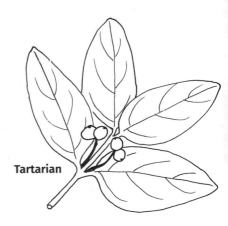

Tartarian

Invasive species (fr R except as noted):
Tartarian, *tatarica*; to 10'; mostly N ½
Amur, *macki*; to 20'; mostly TH
Morrow's, *morrowii*; fr O (R); 6–12';
mostly TH

MINT FAMILY
Beautyberry, *Calicarpa americana*
Fr rose–pink, rose–P, blu;
tightly clustered at axil;
H to 10'; S ½

OLIVE FAMILY
Devilwood

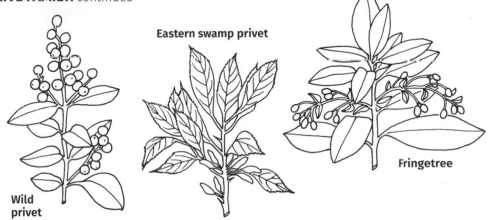

Eastern swamp privet

Fringetree

Wild privet

Fruit	Position	Species	Height	Range
Bla	Terminal panicle	**Wild privet,** *Ligustrum vulgare*	to 16'	TH
P–bla	Small axillary cluster	**Eastern swamp privet,** *Foresteria acuminata*	25–35'	S ½
P–bla	Small axillary cluster	**Devilwood,** *Osmanthus americanus*	to 50'	Coastal LA–VA
P, dark blu, bla	Axils of previous year	**Fringetree,** *Chionanthus virginicus*	to 35'	MO–NY south

MOSCHATEL FAMILY:
Viburnum, Elderberry

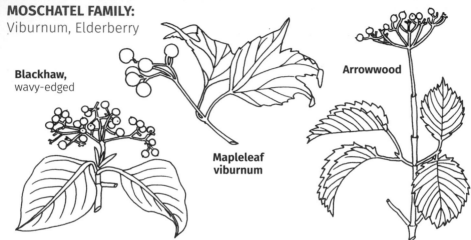

Blackhaw, wavy-edged

Mapleleaf viburnum

Arrowwood

Fruit: drupe	Leaf lobes	Teeth	*Viburnum*	Height	Range
P-Bla	3	Coarse	**Mapleleaf v,** *V. acerfolium*	to 6'	TH
	None	Coarse	**Arrowwood,** *V. dentatum*	to 16'	S ⅔
	None	Fine or wavy	**Blackhaw,** *V. prunifolium*	to 25'	Middle ½
R to dark	None	Fine; lf roundish	**Hobblebush,** *V. lantanoides*	to 10'	TH
	None	Fine; lf egg-shaped	**Nannyberry,** *V. lentago*	to 30'	N ½

20+ viburnums (some with very limited ranges) in eastern North America

Elderberry

Hobblebush
(a viburnum)

Fruit	Panicle	Leaflets	Elderberry *Sambucus*	Height	Range
R	Flat or domed	7 (5–11)	**Black,** *S. nigra*	to 10'	TH
Bla	Pyramidal or domed	5–7	**Red,** *S. racemosa*	to 10'	N ½, GA

Simple Ent/Toothed	W	Y	O	R	P	Blu	Bla	Fruit	Notes		Page
		(Y)		R				Ovoid with silvery scales; lvs with scales		**The "Olives"**	30
E						Blu	Bla	Ellipsoid or spherical	Tree	**Redbay, Sassafras**	38
E				R				Ellipsoid, aromatic	Shrub	**Spicebush**	38
E, T				R				Ellipsoid or longer	Thorny shrub	**Barberry**	39
E					P	Blu	Bla	Spherical to ovoid	Tree	**Tupelo**	39
E				R	P		Bla	Ellipsoid or ovoid	Shrub	**Matrimony vine, bully**	40
E		Y or Y–G						Axillary or terminal	Shrub	**Leatherwood**	41
E	W							On stem, waxy	Shrub	**Laurel family**	41
E		Y–brown						On stem, to 1.5"	Tree	**Persimmon**	42
E					P	Blu	Bla	In domed cluster	To 20'	**Alt-lf dogwood**	28
E, T						Blu	Bla	Seedy; resin dots on lf	Shrub	**Huckleberry**	42
E, T						Blu	Bla	Soft-seeded, juicy	Shrub	**Blueberry, deerberry**	43
(E), T		Y	bright R				Bla	Axillary	Shrub or tree	**Holly family**	44–45
T		(Y)		R	P		Bla	Glossy or whitish	Small tree	**Cherry, plum**	46–47
T				R	P		Bla	Raceme; early fruit	Tree	**Serviceberry**	47
T				R			Bla	Domed-flattened cluster	Shrub	**Chokeberry**	48
T			Salmon O–R				Bla	Solitary, in axil	Tree	**Hackberry**	48
E, T				R			Bla	Solitary or few in axil	Shrub to 20'	**Buckthorn**	49
T		Y		R				Axillary, likely thorny	Shrub-tree	**Hawthorn**	50

Lobed Ent/Toothed	W	Y	O	R	P	Blu	Bla	Fruit	Notes		Page
E						Blu		Pea-size, ellipsoid; red stalk	Tree	**Sassafras**	38
T		(Y)		R				Rounded clusters	Most spp with thorns	**Hawthorn**	50
T				R	P		Bla	Elongate cluster	Shrub; 1 sp spiny	**Currant**	50
T	G			R	P			2 (1–4) in axil	Spiny shrub	**Gooseberry**	50
T				R				Aggregate; (3) 5 lobes	Shrub	**Purple-fl raspberry**	51
T	W				P			Aggregate-like	Tree, lvs 2–4 lobes	**Mulberry**	51
Compound											
T				R			Bla	Aggregate	Stem prickly	**Berry brambles**	37, 52
T				R				Hip; ellipsoid or egg-shaped	Stem prickly	**Rose**	52–53
E, T	W					Do not touch!		Lflts 3, blunt teeth/ shallow lobes		**Poison ivy, oak**	54
E	W							Lflts 7–13		**Poison sumac**	54
T				R				Long, dense column	Shrub, sm tree	**Sumac**	55
T			O	R				Flat-topped cluster	Small tree	**Mountain ash**	55
E		Y						Large panicle	Evergreen tree	**Western soapberry**	56
T		Y						Large panicle in axil	Deciduous tree	**Chinaberry**	56
T				R				In a panicle	Prickly shrub	**Devil's walkingstick**	57

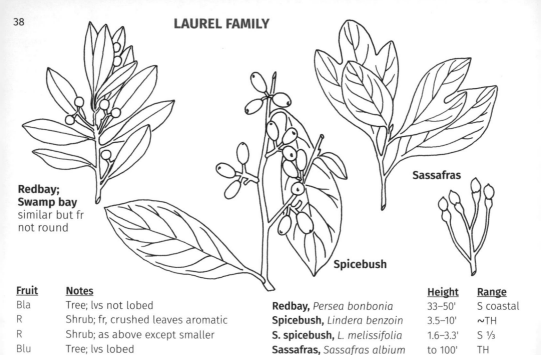

LAUREL FAMILY

Sassafras

**Redbay;
Swamp bay**
similar but fr
not round

Spicebush

Fruit	Notes		Height	Range
Bla	Tree; lvs not lobed	**Redbay,** *Persea bonbonia*	33–50'	S coastal
R	Shrub; fr, crushed leaves aromatic	**Spicebush,** *Lindera benzoin*	3.5–10'	~TH
R	Shrub; as above except smaller	**S. spicebush,** *L. melissifolia*	1.6–3.3'	S ⅓
Blu	Tree; lvs lobed	**Sassafras,** *Sassafras albium*	to 100'	TH

BARBERRY FAMILY: Fruit red, ovoid

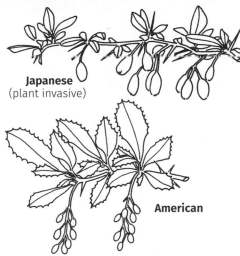

Japanese
(plant invasive)

American

DOGWOOD FAMILY: Tupelo, *Nyssa*

Black, *N. sylvatica*; fr blu–bla, round to ovoid; H to 100' TH
Water, *N. aquatica*; fr P, oblong, ovoid, or ellipsoid; H to 100' S ½
Swamp, *N. biflora*; fr dark P; tree base buttressed; floodplains, swamps; H 50–100'; S ⅓

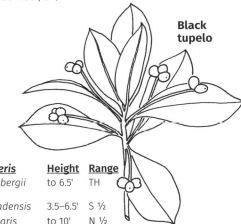

Black tupelo

Leaves	Fruit	Barberry *Berberis*	Height	Range
Entire	Ovoid, solitary or umbel-like cluster of 2–4	**Japanese,** *B. thunbergii*	to 6.5'	TH
Tiny teeth	Ovoid; raceme of ~5–10	**American,** *B. canadensis*	3.5–6.5'	S ½
Tiny teeth	Flat ovoid; raceme of ~10–20	**European,** *B. vulgaris*	to 10'	N ½

Matrimony vine
Lycium barbarum
Fr R, ovoid or ellipsoid;
straggling shrub; H 3.5–20'; TH

**Bully
(bumilia)**

Eastern leatherwood
Dirca palustris
Fr pale Y–G, ellipsoid;
H 3.5–6.5'; TH

Bully: Fruit varies in shape; in clusters at nodes; H to 20'; S ½

Fruit	**Leaves**	**Bully** *Sideroxylon*
Purplish–bla	Smooth below	**Buckthorn,** S. lycioides
Bla	Woolly below	**Gum,** S. lanuginosum

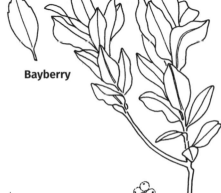

Bayberry

Bayberry and Waxmyrtle
Fr W or bluish–W, waxy, solitary or clusters, on stem; lvs waxy;
bayberry sometimes with a few teeth at lf tip

Leaves	_Morella_	Height	Range
Deciduous	**Northern b,** _M. pensylvanica_	6–10'	Northeast US, Canada
Evergreen	**Southern b,** _M. caroliensis_	6–10'	S ⅓ coastal
Semi-persistent	**Waxmyrtle,** _M. cerifera_	15–20'	S ⅓

Common persimmon
Diospyros virginiana
Fr yellowish–brown, to 1.5" thick;
H 50'; S ⅔

HEATH FAMILY

Huckleberry
Fruit with 10 seed-like
nutlets; lvs resin-dotted
(hand lens useful for
viewing); sometimes
with teeth at lf tip

__Fruit__	__Huckleberry__ *Gaylussacia*		__Height__	__Range__
Bla	**Black ,** *G. baccata*		3.5'	~TH
Bla, hairy	**Dwarf,** *G. dumosa*		6.5'	On/near coastal plain
Dark blu, glaucous	**Blue,** *G. frondosa*		6.5'	Coastal plain MA to SC

HEATH FAMILY: *continued*
Blueberry and Deerberry
Twigs often zigzag, replete with small warts;
lvs toothed, untoothed, or both according to
species; seeds soft

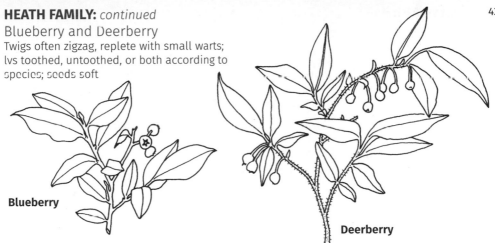

Blueberry

Deerberry

Some common species

Fruit	Leaf margin	*Vaccinium*	Height	Range
Blu–glaucous to bla	Toothed or not	**Highbush b,** *V. corymbosum*	3.5–10'	~TH
Blu–glaucous	Finely toothed	**Lowbush b,** *V. angustifolium*	4"–2'	Northeast
Blu–glaucous	Entire	**Hillside b,** *V. pallidum*	8"–3.3'	TH
Yellowish, greenish, blu	Entire	**Deerberry,** *V. stamineum*	5'	LA–MO to coast, N to NY, Ont

44 HOLLY FAMILY

Fruit in axil; teeth, if present,
on upper half of leaf

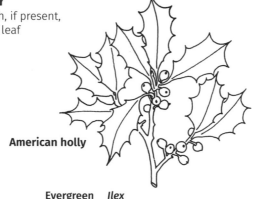

American holly

Fruit	Teeth	Evergreen	*Ilex*	Height	Range
Tree					
R	Spine-tipped	Yes	**American h,** *I. opaca*	to 50'	S ⅔
Shrubs					
Bla	Few at tip	Yes	**Inkberry,** *I. glabra*	3.5–10'	Coastal states
Bla	Few at tip	Yes	**Large gallberry,** *I. coriacea*	to 16'	S coastal states
R	Wavy-edged	Yes	**Yaupon,** *I. vomitoria*	5–15'	S ½
R	Few at tip or none	No	**Mountain h,** *I. montana*	6–20'	Eastern: GA–NY
R	Many small teeth	No	**Common winterberry,** *I. verticillata*	to 15'	TH

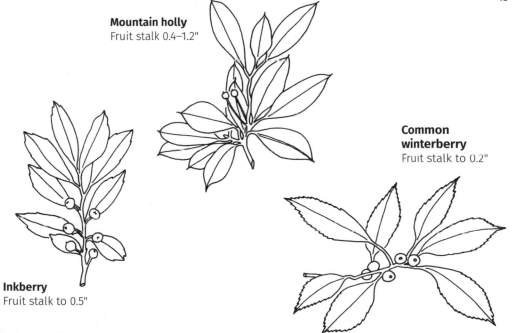

Mountain holly
Fruit stalk 0.4–1.2"

Common winterberry
Fruit stalk to 0.2"

Inkberry
Fruit stalk to 0.5"

Pin cherry

Sand cherry

Some widely distributed species

Fruit 20+ in dense terminal cluster	*Prunus*	**Height**	**Range**
Dark P, bla	**Black cherry,** P. serotina	to 80'	TH
Dark R, bla	**Chokecherry,** P. virginiana	to 30'	N ½
To 12 per umbel-like cluster			
Nearly bla	**Sand cherry,** P. pumila	3' (–9')	N ½
R	**Pin cherry,** P. pensylvanica	to 15'	N ½

Plum:
Stone flattened; fruit solitary or in umbels in axils

Serviceberry (Shadbush, Juneberry):
Fruit with 10 tiny seeds in terminal clusters on new growth; plant flowers early, sets fruit June to midsummer; H shrub to ~50', ~TH

Fruit	Lf underside	*Amelanchier*
P–Bla, dryish	Woolly	**Common s,** A. arborea
P–Bla, juicy	Smooth	**Allegheny s,** A. laevis

This plant blooms when shad run in the spring and fruits in June, when burial services can be held when (in the north) the ground has thawed and dried.

Fruit 0.8" or larger	Plum *Prunus*	Height	Range
R, P–R	**Wild,** P. americana	15–25'	TH
R to Y	**Wild-goose,** P. munsioniana	3.3–33'	S ½
Fruit to 0.6"			
Dark P	**Beach,** P. maritima	3–8'	Coastal ME–VA
R to Y	**Chickasaw,** P. angustifolia	14–25'	S ⅔

ROSE FAMILY: Chokeberry
Base of leaf midrib on top surface with tiny raised glands

Fruit	Aronia	Height	Range
Bright R	**Red,** A. arbutifolia	6–12'	All but Midwest
Bla	**Black,** A. melanocarpa	3–6'	TH
P	**Purple,** A. X prunifolia	8–12'	Eastern US, Canada

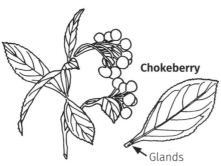

Chokeberry

Glands

HEMP FAMILY: Hackberry

Fruit	Shape	Leaf margin	Hackberry Celtis	Height	Range
Dark O–R	Round	Entire	**Sugar,** C. laevigata	to 100'	S ⅔
Dark R, bla	Ellipsoid to roundish	Toothed	**Common,** C. occidentalis	20–50'	TH
Salmon	Roundish	Toothed	**Dwarf,** C. tenuifolia	to 16'	S ⅔

Common hackberry

BUCKTHORN FAMILY

Alderleaf buckthorn

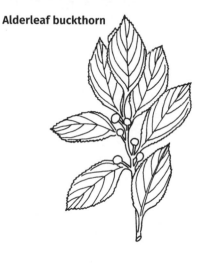

European buckthorn
(some twigs sharp-tipped)

Fruit	Structure	Leaves	Teeth	Buckthorn *Rhamnas*	Height	Range
Bla	Umbel	Opp, sub-opp, alt	Very fine	**European,** *R. cathartica*	to 20'	N ⅔
Bla	Umbel	Alt	Very fine	**Alderleaf,** *R. alnifolia*	3.5–6.5'	N ½
Bla	Mostly solitary	Alt	Very fine	**Lanceleaf,** *R. lanceolata*	3.5–10'	S ⅔

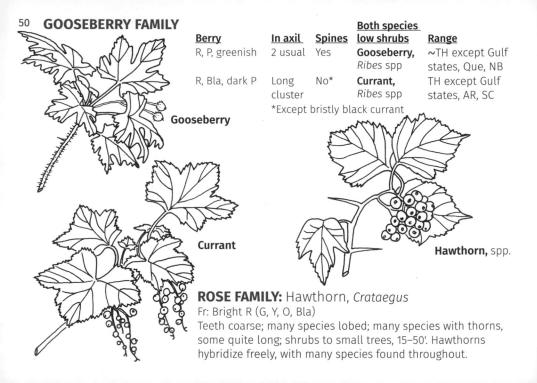

Berry	In axil	Spines	Both species low shrubs	Range
R, P, greenish	2 usual	Yes	**Gooseberry,** *Ribes* spp	~TH except Gulf states, Que, NB
R, Bla, dark P	Long cluster	No*	**Currant,** *Ribes* spp	TH except Gulf states, AR, SC

*Except bristly black currant

Gooseberry

Currant

Hawthorn, spp.

ROSE FAMILY: Hawthorn, *Crataegus*
Fr: Bright R (G, Y, O, Bla)
Teeth coarse; many species lobed; many species with thorns, some quite long; shrubs to small trees, 15–50'. Hawthorns hybridize freely, with many species found throughout.

ROSE FAMILY
Purple-flowering raspberry
Rubus odoratus
Fr R; shrub (not bramble);
no thorns; H 3.5–6.5'; mostly
S mts through Northeast

MULBERRY FAMILY		**Height**	**Range**
Dark P	**Red m,** *Morus rubra*	to 70'	TH
P, cultivars W	**White m,** *Morus alba*	to 50'	TH

ROSE FAMILY: Prickly brambles

When picked, a raspberry separates from the plant easily, leaving the central receptacle behind. A blackberry comes away with the receptacle. Rose has an entirely different structure.

Fruit an aggregate		Cane	Stem	
Separates easily	R	Arching	Round	**Raspberry,** *Rubus* spp
	Bla	Arching	Round	**Black raspberry,** *R. occidentalis*
Does not separate	Deep R to bla	Trailing	Round or angular	**Dewberry,** *Rubus* spp
	Bla	Arching	Angular	**Blackberry,** *Rubus* spp
Fruit a hip	R	Mostly arching	Angular	**Rose,** *Rosa* spp

Some common species:

American red raspberry, *R. idaeus*; N ½

Black raspberry, *R. occidentalis*; N ⅔

Dwarf red raspberry, *R. pubescens*; N ½ (prostrate, from p. 12)

Northern dewberry, *R. flagellaris*; TH

Southern dewberry, *R. trivalis*; S ½

Sawtooth blackberry, *R. argutus*; S ⅔

Pennsylvania blackberry, *R. pensylvanicus*; ~TH

Multiflora rose, *Rosa multiflora* ~20 small hips per cluster; massed thickets to 10–15'; highly invasive; TH

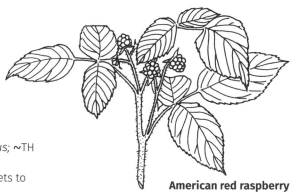

American red raspberry

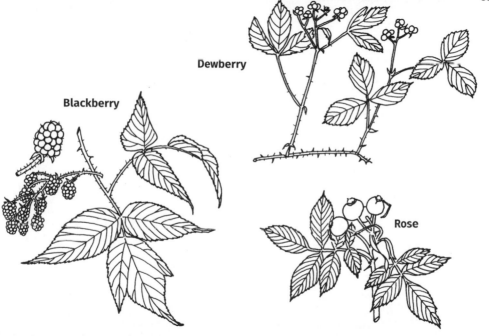

Dewberry

Blackberry

Rose

Poison sumac

Poison ivy
(aerial rootlets)

**DO NOT TOUCH ANY
PART OF PLANT!**

Poison oak

All shrubs; *T. radicans* may also be a vine

7–13 leaflets, entire	*Toxicodendron*	Height	Range
W	**Poison sumac,** *T. vernix*	15'	~TH
3 leaflets, entire, toothed and/or lobed			
Grayish W	**Poison ivy,** *T. radicans*	Climbs	TH
W to yellowish	**Western p.i.,** *T. rydbergii*	3.5–6.5+'	N ½
Tannish W	**Poison oak,** *T. pubescens*	2–4'	S ½

Fruit	Twig hairs	Mountain Ash	*Sorbus*	Height	Range
R	No	**American,**	*S. americana*	30' (–50')	N ⅓, mts
R	No	**Northern,**	*S. decora*	to 30'	N ⅓
R	Yes	**European,**	*S. aucuparia*	to 30'	N ½

ROSE FAMILY: Mountain Ash

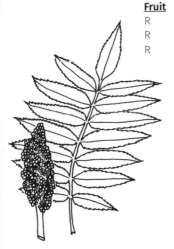

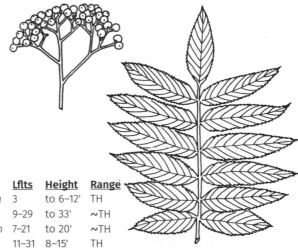

Sumac

Fruit	Hairs on fruit	*Rhus*	Lflts	Height	Range
R	Dense	**Fragrant,** *R. aromatica*	3	to 6–12'	TH
R	Dense	**Staghorn,** *R. thyphina*	9–29	to 33'	~TH
R	Sparse	**Shining,** *R. copallinum*	7–21	to 20'	~TH
R	None	**Smooth,** *R. glabra*	11–31	8–15'	TH

Western soapberry,
Evergreen tree

Chinaberry tree,
Invasive

Fruit	Arrangement	Lf length		Height	Range
Y	Axillary panicle	8–18"	**Chinaberry,** *Melia azedarch*	20–40'	S ½
Y	Terminal panicle	to 12"	**Western soapberry,** *Sapindus saponaria*	30–40'	~S ¼
Bla	Umbel, red stems	to 3.3'	**Devil's walkingstick,** *Aralia spinosa*	10–15'	~S ⅔, NY, PA

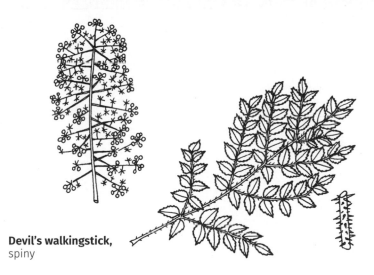

Devil's walkingstick,
spiny

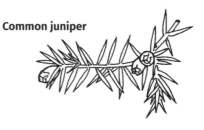

Common juniper

American yew

From p. 12
Creeping juniper

Fruit	**Needles**		**Height**	**Range**
Bright R	Single	**American yew,** *Taxus canadensis*	Shrub	N ⅔
		Juniperus		
Blu, bla	Whorls of 3	**Common juniper,** *J. communis*	2–6.5'	N ⅔
Blu	Mostly opposite	**Creeping juniper,** *J. horizontals*	Prostrate	N ⅓
Blu, glaucous	Mostly opposite	**Eastern red cedar,** *J. virginiana*	to 66'	TH

Palmetto, spp

Fruit	*Sabal*	Height	Range
Bla	**Cabbage palmetto,** *S. palmetto*	40–50'	S ¼
Bla	**Dwarf palmetto,** *S. minor*	5–10'	S ⅓

Eastern red cedar

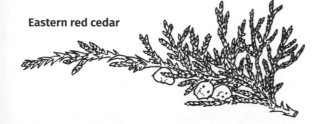

INDEX

Amelanchier, **36**, 47
Ampelopsis, **5**, 6–7
Aralia, spp, **18**, 22
 spinosa, **37**, 57
Arcstaphyloss, **12**, 13
Arisaema, **18**, 24
Aronia, **37**, 48
Arrowwood, **22**, 34
Asparagus, 4
Autumn olive, **36**, 30

Baneberry, **18**, 25
Barberry, **36**, 39
Bayberry, **36**, 41
Bearberry, **12**, 13
Beautyberry, **26**, 32
Belacandra, **14**, 17
Berberis, **36**, 39
Berchemia, **5**, 9
Bittersweet, **5**, 11
Blackberry, **37**, 52–3
Blue bead lily, **14**, 17
Blueberry, **36**, 43
Buckthorn, **26**, 36, 49

Buffaloberry, **18**, 30
Bunchberry, **12**, **26**, 28–9
Bully, **36**, 40

Calicarpa, **26**, 32
Calla, **18**, 24
Calyocarpum, **5**, 10
Carrionflower, **5**, 8
Caulophyllum, **18**, 25
Celastrus, **5**, 11
Celtis, **36**, 48
Chenopodium, **18**, 20
Cherry, **36**, 46
Cherry, ground, **18**, 20
Chinaberry, **37**, 56
Chionanthus, **26**, 33
Chokeberry, **36**, 48
Clintonia, **14**, 17
Cocculus, **5**, 10
Cohosh, **18**, 25
Convaliaria, **14**, 16
Cornus, **12**, **18**, **26**, 28–9
Coralberry, **26**, 27
Cranberry, **12**, 13
Cranberrybush, **26**, 34

Crataegus, **36–7**, 50
Cucumber-root, **14**, 17
Cupseed, **5**, 10
Currant, **37**, 50

Deerberry, **36**, 43
Devil's walkingstick, **37**, 57
Devilwood, **26**, 32
Dewberry, **37**, 52–3
Diospyros, **36**, 42
Dirca, **36**, 41
Dogwood, **26**, 28–9, **36**

Elaeagnus, **26**, 30
Elderberry, **26**, 35

Fairybells, **14**, 15
Foresteria, **26**, 33
Fragaria, **12**, 12
Fringetree, **26**, 33

Gaultheria, **12**, 13
Gaylussacia, **36**, 42
Ginsing, **18**, 22
Goldenseal, **18**, 20
Gooseberry, **36**, 50
Grape, **5**, 6–7
Green dragon, **18**, 24

Greenbriar, **5**, 8

Hackberry, **36**, 48
Hawthorn, **36–7**, 50
Hedera, **5**, 11
Hobblebush, **26**, 34–5
Holly, **36**, 44–45
Honeysuckle vine, **5**, 9
 shrub, **26**, 31
Horse-gentian, **18**, 19
Horsenettle, **18**, 19
Huckleberry, **36**, 42
Hydrastis, **18**, 20

Ilex, **36**, 44–5
Indica strawberry, **12**, 13
Inkberry, **36**, 44–5
Ivy, English, **5**, 11

Jack in the pulpit, **18**, 24
Juniper, *Juniperus*, 58

Leatherwood, **36**, 40
Ligustrum, **26**, 33
Lilium, **14**, 16
Lily, blackberry, **14**, 17
 tiger, **14**, 16
Lily of the valley, **14**, 16

Lindera, **36**, 38
Lonicera, vine, **5**, 9
  shrub, **26**, 31
Lycium, **36**, 40

Maianthemum, **14**, 15–6
Mandarin, nodding, **14**
Matrimony vine, **36**, 40
Mayflower, Canada, **14**, 16
Medeola, **14**, 17
Melia, **37**, 56
Menispermum, **5**, 10
Mitchella, **12**, 13
Mockstrawberry, **12**, 12
Moonseed, **5**, 10
Morella, **36**, 41
Morus, **37**, 51
Mountain-ash, **37**, 55
Mulberry, **37**, 51

Nannyberry, **26**, 34
Nightshade, **18**, 21
Nyssa, **36**–7, 39

Osmanthus, **26**, 33

Palmetto, 59
Panax, **18**, 22

Parthenocissus, **5**, 6
Partridgeberry, **12**, 12
Peppervine, **5**, 6–7
Persea, **36**, 38
Persimmon, **36**, 42
Physalis, **18**, 20
Phytolacca, **18**, 19
Plum, *Prunus*, **36**, 47
Poison ivy, **5**, **37**, 54
  oak, sumac, **37**, 54
Pokeweed, **18**, 19
Polygonatum, **14**, 14
Porcelainberry, **5**, 6
Potentilla, **12**, 13
Privet, **26**, 33
Prosartes, **14**, 15
Prunus spp, **36**–7, 46–7
  odoratus, **36**–7, 51
  pubescens, **12**, 52

Raspberry, **37**, 52
  dwarf, **13**, 52
  purple-fl, **37**, 51
Redbay, **36**, 38
Rhamnas, **26**, **36**, 49
Rhus, **37**, 55

Ribes, **37**, 50
Rose, **37**, 52–3
Rubus brambles, **37**, 52–53
  odoratus, **37**, 51
  pubescens, **13**, 52
Russian olive, **22**, 38

Sabal, 59
Sambucus, **26**, 35
Sapindus, **37**, 56
Sarsaparilla, **18**, 22–3
Sassafras, **36**–7, 38
Serviceberry, **36**, 47
Shepherdia, **26**, 30
Sideroxylon, **36**, 40
Silverberry, **26**, 30
Smilax, **5**, 8
Snowberry, **26**, 27
Snowberry, creeping, **12**, 13
Soapberry, **37**, 56
Solanum, **18**, 21
Solomon's seal, **14**, 14
Solomon's seal, false, **14**, 15

Sorbus, **37**, 55
Spicebush, **36**, 38
Spikenard, **18**, 23
Strawberry, **12**, 12
Strawberry-blight, **18**, 20
Streptopus, **14**, 14
Sumac, **37**, 55
Supplejack, **5**, 9
Symphoricarpos, **26**, 27

Taxus, **58**, 58
Toxicodendron, **37**, 54
Trillium, **18**, 19
Triostium, **18**, 19
Tupelo, **36**, 39
Twisted stalk, **14**, 14

Vaccinium, **13**, **36**, 43
Viburnum, **26**, 34–5
Virginia creeper, **5**, 6
Vitis, **5**, 6–7

Waxmyrtle, **36**, 41
Winterberry, **36**, 44–5
Wintergreen, **12**, 13
Wolfberry, **26**, 27

Other books in the pocket-size *Finder* series:

FOR US AND CANADA EAST OF THE ROCKIES

Bird Finder frequently seen birds

Bird Nest Finder aboveground nests

Fern Finder native ferns of the Midwest and Northeast

Flower Finder spring wildflowers & flower families

Life on Intertidal Rocks organisms of the North Atlantic Coast

Scat Finder mammal scat

Track Finder mammal tracks and footprints

Tree Finder native and common introduced trees

Winter Tree Finder leafless winter trees

Winter Weed Finder dry plants in winter

FOR STARGAZERS

Constellation Finder patterns in the night sky and star stories

FOR FORAGERS

Mushroom Finder fungi of North America

Dorcas S. Miller, founding president of the Maine Master Naturalist Program, has written more than a dozen books, including *Scat Finder, Winter Weed Finder, Berry Finder, Bird Nest Finder*, and *Constellation Finder*. Her *Finder* books have sold more than half a million copies.

NATURE STUDY GUIDES are published by AdventureKEEN, 2204 1st Ave. S., Suite 102, Birmingham, AL 35233; 800-678-7006; naturestudy.com. See shop.adventurewithkeen.com for our full line of nature and outdoor activity guides by ADVENTURE PUBLICATIONS, MENASHA RIDGE PRESS, and WILDERNESS PRESS, including many guides for birding, wildflowers, rocks, and trees, plus regional and national parks, hiking, camping, backpacking, and more.